CW01306021

"The lay out is 'happy', positive and encourages interaction. The message is both useful and practical and I think the summary 'Takeaway' sections are particularly valuable. There's a pick 'n mix thing I like about this book. When I'm time constrained, I can turn to a section relevant to my day and absorb it. Easy to use and an advance on my productivity and co-worker collaboration."

Will Hanrahan, Creative Director, First Look TV

"Genius Learning have a unique knack of providing powerful learning experiences in interesting ways that challenge, excite and ignites creative sparks in learners. They are leaders in their field and their purpose shines through in every email, call, session or meeting (virtual or otherwise!). They are energisers and they're shakers, they are challengers and cheerleaders and they are people champions and impact creators. If you have a tricky issue to unpick or want to elevate from good to great, I whole heartedly recommend Genius Learning."

James Gilfoyle, Organisational Learning & Development Manager, Edge Hill University

"The team at Genius Learning have always stood out from the crowd. They have a high level of behavioural intelligence and this is something that draws results. Be it the ability to gauge emotion, to empower, to nurture the ideas in the back of your mind or to support you on a personal or organisational journey.
David Morris, Non-Financial Risk Training and Engagement Specialist, Deutsche Bank

DOWNLOAD

OUR FREE WORKSHEETS TO SUPPORT YOUR LEARNING HERE

www.inspireyourgenius.com/books/

Caroline Esterson & Wendy Gannaway
YOUR GENIUS IDEAS BOOK
A dose of commercial creativity for busy L&D professionals

© 2020, Caroline Esterson & Wendy Gannaway
Self-published
ISBN: 9798664968538
caroline@inspireyourgenius.com
www.inspireyourgenius.com

All rights reserved.
No part of this publication may be reproduced, stored in a retrieval system, stored in a database and / or published in any form or by any means, electronic, mechanical, photocopying, recording or otherwise, without the prior written permission of the publisher.

We are facing unprecedented times of change and never before has L&D been under so much pressure.
AND, of course, it is also a massive opportunity to shine.

Let this book guide your thinking and support you to help the people in your organisation thrive.

Use it to scribble, doodle, make notes and colour in to allow space for your thinking to deepen.

After all, when your people GROW, success FLOWS

YOUR GENIUS IDEAS BOOK
A dose of commercial creativity for busy L&D professionals

By Caroline Esterson & Wendy Gannaway,
Genius Learning Ltd

Contents

PART ONE: INTRODUCTION — **Page 1**
L&D under pressure — Page 2
What does disruption means to you? — Page 3
Where do you get your best ideas? — Page 5
The Importance of Reflection — Page 7
Peak and Flow — Page 9

PART TWO: BEING THE BEST YOU CAN BE — **Page 14**
How are you now? — Page 16
Adopt a DotCom mindset — Page 18
What do you believe about others? — Page 20
Becoming a Learning Entrepreneur — Page 22
Supercharge your credibility — Page 29

PART THREE:
MOVING TOWARDS A LEARNING ORGANISATION — **Page 34**
What is a Learning Organisation? — Page 35
Why is it important to move towards a Learning Organisation? — Page 36
A better future: Your Learning Strategy — Page 39
A Better Normal: Integrated Learning — Page 41
Your vision for learning — Page 45
Tips for engaging stakeholders — Page 48

PART FOUR: ENGAGING LEARNERS — **Page 53**
Creating an engaging user experience — Page 55
Principle 1: Follow the full Learning Cycle — Page 58
Principle 2: Get into the Learning Zone — Page 61
Principle 3: Keep it SAVI — Page 64
Principle 4: Promote Discovery — Page 67
Principle 5: Mirror Real Life — Page 70
Principle 6: Set Up, Stand Back, Pull Together — Page 73
Principle 7: Layer Learning — Page 76
Principle 8: Offer learning through CPR — Page 79

PART FIVE: PULLING IT ALL TOGETHER — **Page 84**
Time for action — Page 85
Challenge Time — Page 86
Go for it: Your commitments — Page 88
Enjoy your success — Page 89

OUT OF CONFUSION comes CLARITY

PART ONE:
Introduction

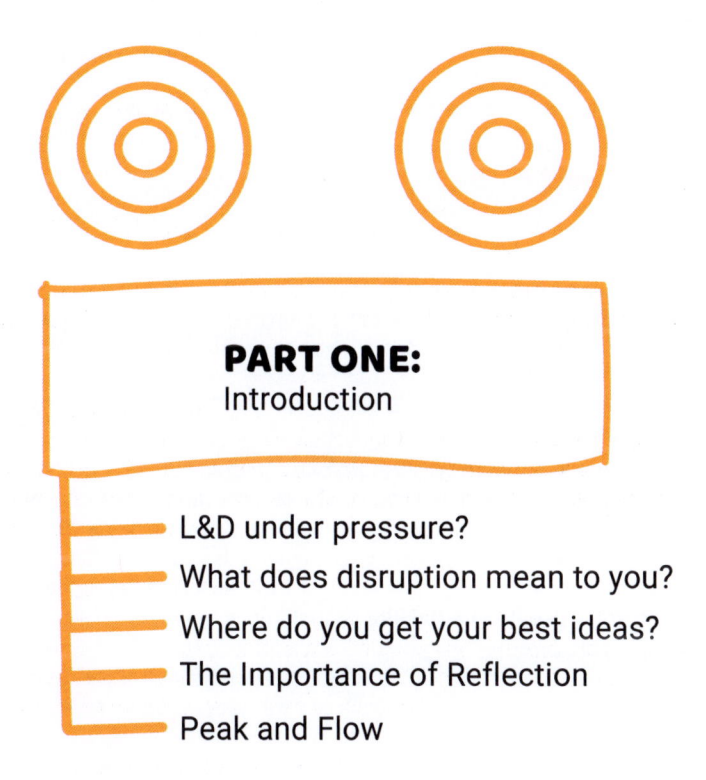

- L&D under pressure?
- What does disruption mean to you?
- Where do you get your best ideas?
- The Importance of Reflection
- Peak and Flow

L&D under pressure

Never before has L&D been under so much pressure. AND, of course, it is also a massive opportunity to shine.

We are in the midst of a health, social and economic emergency. Organisations are struggling. Your learning; its strategy and deployment, can play a significant role in supporting your organisation to be one of the ones to succeed, despite this turbulence.

The organisations that thrive are the ones that have a culture that has moved from people defining themselves as experts (knowing it all and putting on a good show) to those who want to collaborate and solve problems (trying to understand the challenges, embrace learning and experimentation). They have created a culture that is the epitome of a Learning Organisation.

Your organisation needs leaders at all levels, in all functions to step up and shape the future of work. It is those people who can embrace and perform against the backdrop of uncertainty and are able to explore ideas and solutions with open curiosity who will win the day.

This is one of those significant opportunities for people to step up and take the lead. L&D has the ability to touch everyone in the organisation so we all need to lead from the front. Whether you are an L&D professional working inside or outside an organisation, this book will help elevate your thinking. If you are leading a team of L&D Professionals, this book will support you to stretch, challenge and shape your team to be role model leaders of learning.

What does disruption mean to you?

There is much talk about being disruptive. Disruption is all around us... from new start-ups seizing dramatic market share almost overnight from the big boys; in parenting exploring how to raise a child in today's ever-changing world and in food with new chefs mixing sensual pleasures that ensures their restaurants are booked a year in advance.

But what about learning?
The L&D profession is no exception. L&D has undergone major disruption in the past decade yet many organisations are still struggling to adapt and make the most of the opportunities that disruption provides.

Think about the learning you provide. How well does it equip staff in your organisation to respond quickly to the pressures of the external climate? Do you, perhaps, need to be more disruptive?

From CEO's to Learning professionals the consensus is that organisations lack critical skills to combat the challenges of today let alone those of the future. We need to work better and smarter. But how are YOU responding to this call to action?

What does disruption mean to L&D right now in your role?

Share some of your thinking on our Facebook group to engage in the debate: facebook.com/groups/learningentrepreneurs

Thank you.

Thank you for answering the questions on the previous page. It's an important place to start and be honest with ourselves. Even before the pandemic, in many organisations L&D was struggling. Struggling to keep up with demand. Struggling to effect a change. Struggling to deliver real value that moved the dials in business. In a lot of organisations L&D was seen as a 'nice to have' rather than a 'must have' and one of the first casualties of cost-cutting measures. But it doesn't have to be that way...anymore! The pandemic has provided L&D with an opportunity for change and it's crucial to seize that opportunity. In doing so you will build your credibility, offer incredible opportunities for people to develop themselves and provide real commercial value that helps your organisation thrive.

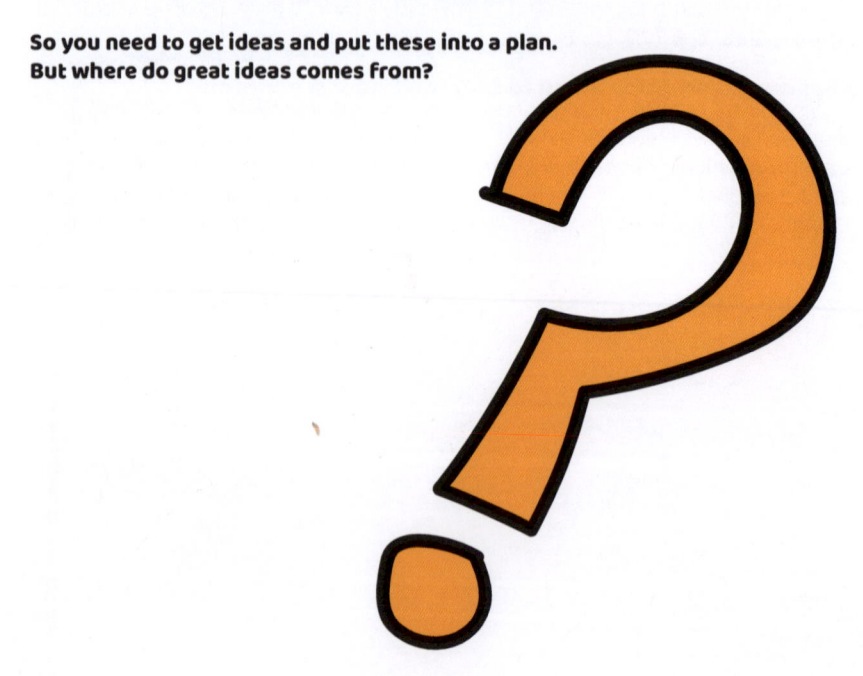

**So you need to get ideas and put these into a plan.
But where do great ideas comes from?**

Where do you get your best ideas?

We are frequently asked where we get our ideas from and never do we answer *'when we are on our computers'*. Sometimes it's in the shower, when on a dog walk or when inspired by a TV programme. Never when we are forcing it. We have learnt over time that even when we are maxed out with competing demands, we need to take time out in order to grow and be creative for our clients. We have developed a discipline that allows us the time to be creative. We build in that time each day to allow ideas to flow.

In today's crazy world where your 'to do list' is 10 pages long and your schedule is back to back meetings this can be a tough ask. We understand this. Yet, we all have the same amount of time, it's what we choose to do with our time that matters. Also know that it can be done if you BELIEVE it's important. If you WANT it enough!

Learning & Development by its very nature needs to be curious.
As L&D professionals, you need to continuously explore new ways of doing things and be prepared to actively encourage others to do the same.

Your organisation will never create their 'better normal' by deploying the same actions as they did before. You will never gain the traction to move your organisation without taking time to reflect on your experiences and seek out new ways of tackling your challenges.

Ideas in Action

In the book **"Where Good Ideas Come From: The Natural History of Innovation"** by Steve Johnson, there are 5 key ideas that are worth you pondering on here.

There is very little under the sun that is totally new.
Most new ideas come from rearranging or reconnecting things in a different way. That is why taking time out for reflection is so important to help you do just that.

Eureka!
"Eureka!" moments, when the light bulb supposedly goes on instantly and the idea sparks into life in the mind of the discoverer, are mostly fictional. Instead, the discovery usually comes at the end of a long series of near-discoveries. So reflection helps you catalogue your thoughts and short-circuit this ideas gestation time.

Serendipity
The happy accidents that allow creativity to flourish are often not entirely accidental. Some innovators conduct themselves in a way that encourages happy accidents. The more you set out your intentions, the more your unconscious mind is open to triggers that will support you in your endeavours.

New ideas that take off come from "just next door" or "the adjacent possible".
If the idea is too new, with too many unfamiliar components, then the world isn't ready for it: the timing isn't right and the idea has to wait decades or even centuries before it becomes accepted. So if you need to really challenge the norm in your organisation, reflect on the steps you need to go through to help move stakeholders with you.

Sole Inventors are making life difficult
The "sole inventor working alone" is almost a total myth: most new ideas occur in networks of thinkers who are mulling over similar issues. If you want to be creative, get yourselves out there. Engage in debates, comment on social media posts and articles; indeed write them yourself! And of course join us on our facebook group too.

OVER TO YOU!
Bearing this in mind, what action can you take that will help you get more great ideas? List at least 3 places you commit to engage with to explore your thinking deeper. If you're unsure why not ask the Facebook group for recommendations?
facebook.com/groups/learningentrepreneurs

1.

2.

3.

The Importance of Reflection

Reflection encourages you to be honest with yourself; to face up to the challenges you have and to reflect on how well you are tackling them. Reflection is at the heart of self-development.

Being reflective will help your learning, communication and decision-making become more effective. It helps you be honest with yourself.

Success doesn't happen overnight. Just like anything worthwhile you need to practice. Practice results in progress. You need to find the best time and place for you to reflect. For many people this is away from where the 'work' happens. The most important thing is that you carve out time and create a daily habit. The more you practice, the easier and faster it will become.

This book provides you with a place to scribble, doodle and make notes. It is supported by thoughts and ideas to stretch your reflection further to help ensure you are the best version of you that you can be and that the learning you provide really delivers value for individuals and your organisation.

Our mind and body is connected. In our live learning (events and workshops) we have fiddle toys on the tables for those who need 'touch' to help stimulate concentration and thinking. This book takes this to a different level, allowing you to switch off your brain from other thoughts that can distract your focus from being in the moment. It also helps you to get into a relaxed state of awareness which elevates creative and quality thinking.

==And before you start why not join our Facebook group==
www.facebook.com/groups/learningentrepreneurs
so together we can strengthen our insights and solutions to help our organisations thrive.

The Mischievous MUST

If you're anything like us, you will have a huge To-Do list and a host of additional things that don't even make it to the illustrious list! It feels like a tough ask to take time out for reflection. We often say to each other things like those below and despite even jotting it down on the nearest post-it note, often it doesn't get done.

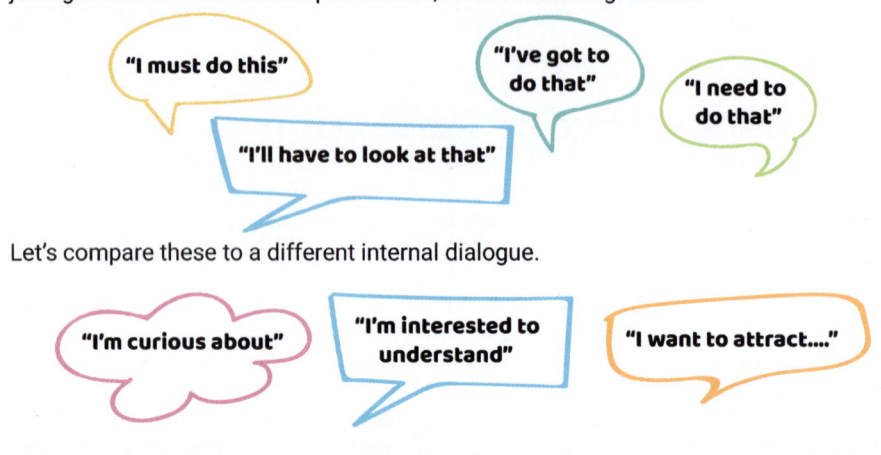

- "I must do this"
- "I've got to do that"
- "I need to do that"
- "I'll have to look at that"

Let's compare these to a different internal dialogue.

- "I'm curious about"
- "I'm interested to understand"
- "I want to attract…."

Which do you think is better?
'Must' and 'need' are verbs associated with necessity. Necessity has an important part to play in our lives, such as nudging us to do things to keep us alive, for example, "I need to have my medicine," "I must have something to eat." In certain circumstances and when overused they can create tension, for instance, "I need to tell my neighbour to stop parking their car in front of my garage," or "I must talk to my manager about my workload."

On the other hand, 'want' is a verb associated with desire. Desire is a potent emotion that will give you immense positive energy. Think about a time when you wanted something or someone so much that you found a way, maybe creatively, to get it/them. And depending on how much you wanted it/them, you didn't give up. And the strangest thing is, when you really want something/someone, it takes on a whole different priority and urgency, often despite not being urgent or important in the grand scheme of things!

'Want' has a different pull to it, one that is enthused with joy and possibility, and as a result puts us into a resourceful state of mind. When we are feeling resourceful, we can think logically and laterally, and are able to get those things on our To-Do lists done, often with effortless ease. We are energised, positively. We can connect the dots, solve problems, see solutions, make recommendations and challenge where appropriate.

The quality of what we do is elevated.
And when that positive energy leaks out in our interactions with others, whether in person, social media or in writing, that's when we become attractive. As L&D professionals, when we operate from a place of desire ("I want to make a difference…") as opposed to necessity ("I need to make a difference…") is when we as L&D are seen within the organisation as a 'must have' rather than a 'nice to have'.

Peak and Flow

Peak state provides you with the energy to make things happen. It provides momentum and allows you to produce great results under pressure. But we don't want every day to be like that, it would be exhausting.

You also need to find flow.

Flow is that state of consciousness where you are so engrossed in whatever you are doing that you become single-minded, lose track of time and just melt into the moment.

Flow is a concept first studied by Mihaly Csíkszentmihályi, a Hungarian psychologist and one of the first pioneers of the scientific study of happiness. According to Csíkszentmihályi, there are a number of factors that accompany the experience of flow. While many of these may be present, it's not necessary to experience all of them for flow to occur:

1. Strong concentration and complete focus on the activity itself and task at hand
2. Clear goals that, while challenging, are attainable
3. The activity is intrinsically rewarding
4. Loss of self-consciousness; forgetting about others and the world around you
5. A distorted sense of time; feeling so focused on the present that you lose track of passing time
6. Immediate feedback; there is a clear set of goals and progress benchmarks to provide direction and structure
7. Perfect balance between skill level and the challenge presented
8. Feelings of personal control over the situation and outcome (as opposed to anxiety)
9. Lack of awareness of physical needs

Flow leads to improved performance and increased productivity.

It promotes learning and skill development, which drives innovation and complex thinking. On an organisational scale, it creates a culture of high performance, empowerment, creativity, and morale.

In order to achieve and maintain the flow state, it's important to seek new challenges and information. Otherwise, apathy sets in and the task becomes monotonous. Furthermore, it's when you are in flow that you achieve true productivity. Flow is about maximising your strengths and leveraging these in your job.

Flow is the state needed for successful reflection.
It is beneficial because your subconscious houses your creativity. You are less likely to hold back due to fear while in flow because you're not "thinking", you're just doing. Most creative people recognise this state and have noticed that when they are in flow their creations (words, paintings, music) seem to stream out of them effortlessly. It's your "Intuitive Assistant" that will become your right-hand when you're working. In our constantly disturbed workplace, whether an open plan office, or at home with other distractions, it can be really tough getting into flow. As L&D professionals it is important that you recognise this. Explore means of enabling yourself to have 'space', both physically and mentally to get into flow through the way your work is organised, planned and implemented.

How to find your flow
Finding flow is not mystical, you don't need to meditate to get in a great state. Flow is highly practical. It takes practice but like everything, the more you practice the better you become. Here are some easy steps you can take to help you:

1. **Find a way to love it**
   Doing something you dread will not induce flow. Start with a task you LOVE and if you don't, find a way to reframe it by focusing on the value you and/or others will get out of you doing a great job.

2. **Make sure it's challenging**
   Select something that challenges you and will force you to concentrate.

3. **Work out when you are most productive**
   We all have best times of day to work really productively. Analyse your energy levels to help you work out when is the best time for you.

4. **Eliminate distractions**
   Silence notifications, turn off music, find a quiet place. All of these will help you get into flow more easily. If you need to stay at a desk, then tidy your desk so your eyes aren't distracted by the papers around you.

5. **Don't set a time limit**
   Allow yourself the luxury of taking as long as it takes without false pressure.

6. **Enjoy yourself**
   Take time to appreciate the simple enjoyment of allowing yourself to be in flow and everything that flows from it.

How can you set yourself up to achieve more flow in work?

Key takeaways

1. Learning and Development professionals need to be curious. If you aren't you shouldn't be in this job - so get curious fast!

2. Great ideas aren't forced when you are behind your computer screen. They come from allowing yourself to experience things. By you noticing, questioning and reflecting on your experiences.

3. There is very little that is totally new. Ideas come from connecting pieces of the jigsaw together and making new connections or understanding.

4. Being reflective will help your learning, communication and decision-making become more effective. It helps you be honest with yourself.

5. The sheer volume of work we need to get through each day means that we work at peak level much of the time. To develop your reflective skills it's important to learn to be in the flow which allows your unconscious mind to explore new ideas.

6. Stop putting pressure on yourself by making things a MUST. Rather than focusing on necessity, find a way for the things you want to stem from desire; from wanting them, really wanting them. That way you will be more motivated to take the necessary action.

"You have brains in your head.
You have feet in your shoes.
You can steer yourself any direction you choose.
You're on your own, and you know what you know.
And you are the one who'll decide where you'll go.
Oh the places you'll go!"
Dr Seuss

Before we move on...

Take a few moments to jot down the thoughts, ideas or actions that have come to you from exploring this section.

PART TWO
BEING THE BEST YOU CAN BE

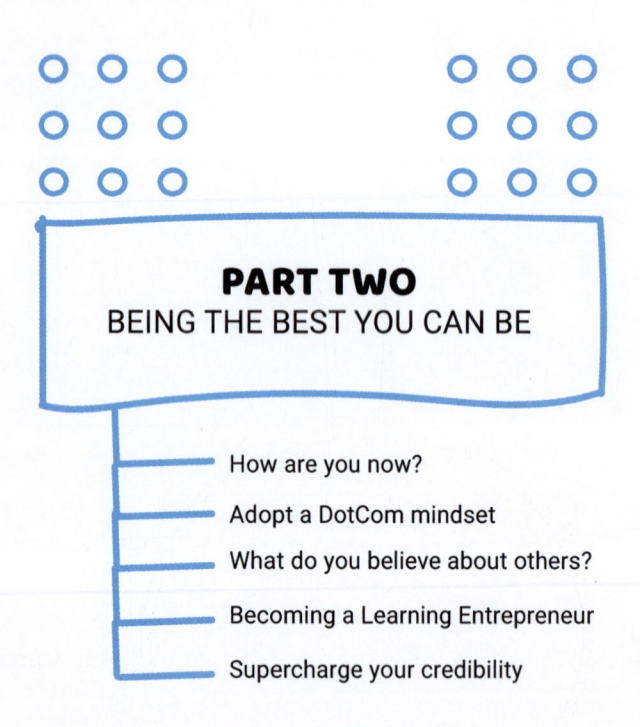

- How are you now?
- Adopt a DotCom mindset
- What do you believe about others?
- Becoming a Learning Entrepreneur
- Supercharge your credibility

Being your best self

You know you are capable of great things but often the sheer busyness of our world gets in the way. Now is the time for action and to start developing great habits that will help you grow.

And in doing so, you will help others too. As a Learning & Development professional remember how many people you touch and can influence. You are a role model to others, make sure you really are the best version of yourself.

How are you now? Self Reflection

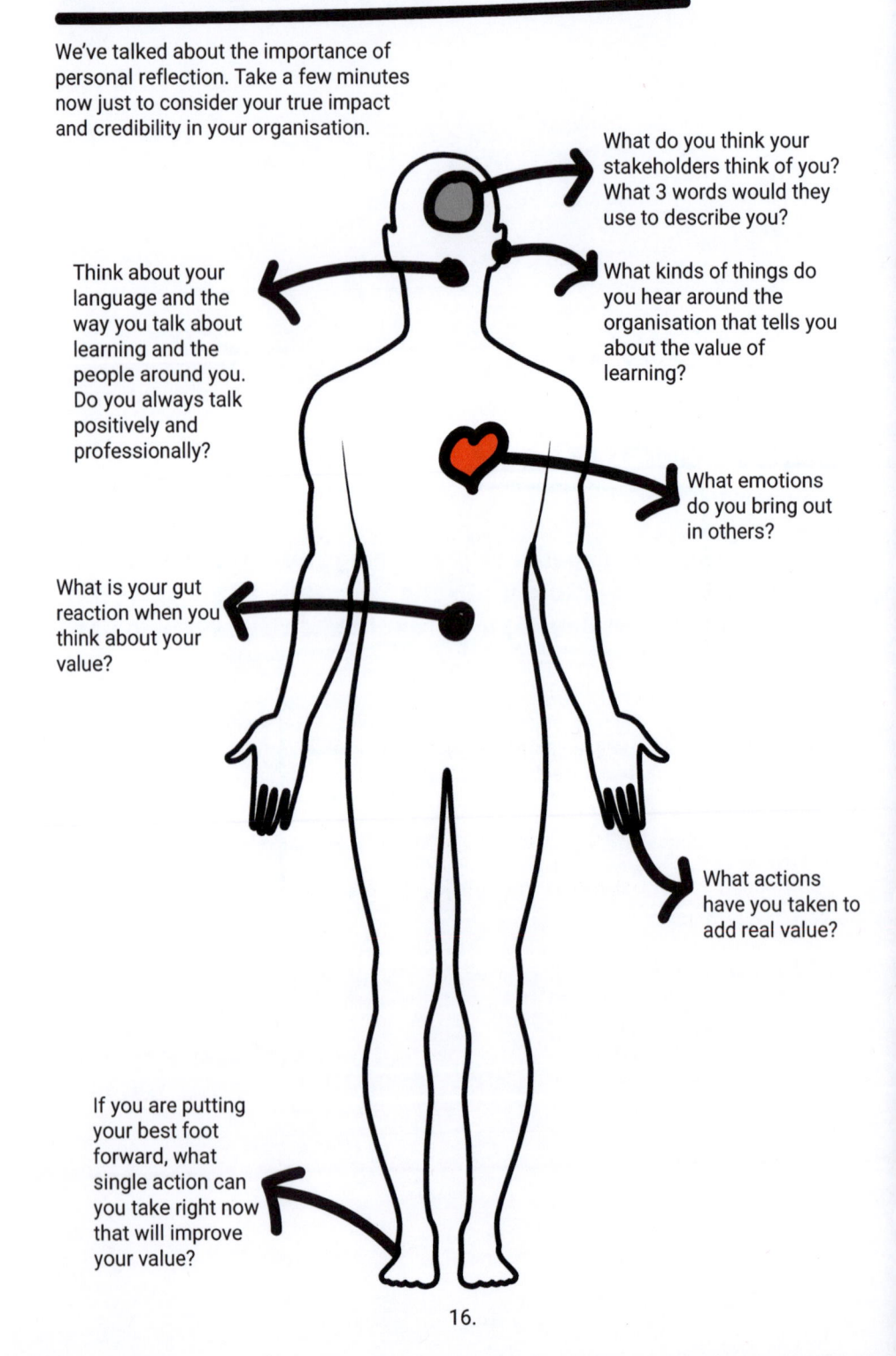

We've talked about the importance of personal reflection. Take a few minutes now just to consider your true impact and credibility in your organisation.

What do you think your stakeholders think of you? What 3 words would they use to describe you?

Think about your language and the way you talk about learning and the people around you. Do you always talk positively and professionally?

What kinds of things do you hear around the organisation that tells you about the value of learning?

What emotions do you bring out in others?

What is your gut reaction when you think about your value?

What actions have you taken to add real value?

If you are putting your best foot forward, what single action can you take right now that will improve your value?

What key improvements can you make now to increase your impact and value?

Does fear hold you back?

Fear of failure is extremely common. Some people talk about the Imposter Syndrome. However you look at it this fear limits your potential. It leads to uncertainty, pain and self-doubt. In fact many high-achievers will share their stories of doubt and fear. The difference is that they've learned how to overcome it and found ways to leverage more positive thoughts and feelings to help them drive forward.

Tony Robbins offers 3 steps for helping you forge a new more empowering pathway to help you succeed.

- **Let go of limiting beliefs**
  This is about the way you talk about yourself and to yourself. You need to analyse the internal dialogue you have and where necessary change it with empowering beliefs that affirm your self-worth and professional skills. If you hear yourself saying "They won't take advice from me" for example, change this to "They need support and I can help them". This will help you learn from personal challenges rather than being enslaved by them.

- **Learn from others**
  There will be people inside and outside your organisation who have stood in your shoes. Find them and learn how they combated their limiting beliefs and forged a new path.

- **Mitigating your risks**
  Through planning you can reduce the risks of stepping up. Allow yourself the time to prepare for every situation you enter that can influence how others experience you. This can be as simple as a few minutes before you have a meeting, focus your mind and picture what a successful outcome will look, sound and feel like for you.

Adopt a DotCom mindset

We know you are skilled, knowledgeable and experienced but we bet you have had times when your ideas have been pushed aside or felt frustrated by the way others have treated you.

Adopting a DotCom mindset can liberate you from frustrations. This mindset shifts your thinking from being an employee to that of a consultant. This is Wendy's story.

I was so frustrated at work until one day I asked someone who I saw as a role model how he managed to navigate through the complex personalities, hidden agendas and general trappings of organisational politics. This person was not a director but was viewed as a person of high influence (and this was in an organisation where status trumped everything). He spoke up, he challenged the status quo, he put forward ideas all without the aggression and attitude that is often associated with people who get heard.

He told me "Simple. I don't consider myself to be an employee. I am a top consultant. I believe myself to be 'DaveSmith.Com' - international troubleshooter brought in especially to save the company. This way I distance myself from the hierarchy and focus on what I need to do to ensure the job gets done...properly!"

This 'Dot Com' mindset thing swam around in my mind and when I woke up the next morning and got ready for work it was as though someone had waved a magic wand and I was liberated. I was now WendyGannaway.Com - highly sought after Learning and Development specialist brought in especially to inspire and help develop the staff to be the best they can be. I no longer reported to a manager - my manager was now one of my clients, along with other line managers and directors who were also clients. I didn't give advice, I made recommendations. I stopped saying what I could do for different departments and developed a positive strategy for learning. I stopped talking about programmes and started talking about solutions. I asked questions, listened and pushed back if I thought something wasn't in their best interest and offered alternative solutions. Slowly I had started to run myself as a business, even to the extent of working out my fees, which I kept a note of privately. And perhaps most importantly, I allowed myself to make mistakes and also to TRUST that good things would come out of even the toughest challenge because I chose to believe that there is no such thing as failure only learning and understanding.

This was a really crucial mindset shift!

Creating a DotCom mindset

1. What do you need to ALLOW yourself?
This is about what you give yourself permission to do. e.g. I'm allowed to make mistakes as long as I learn from them.

2. What do you need to CALL yourself?
This is about your identity e.g. Wonder Woman, International Troubleshooter...

3. What do you need to TELL yourself?
This is about positive affirmations e.g. "You are successful" "You are creative"

As you ponder this....

Think about
- What untapped potential are you still hiding?
- How might the DotCom mindset help you to free it?
- And what benefits could unfold for you, your colleagues, your customers, your family and friends if you were to use it?

What do you believe about others?

Our beliefs about people guide the way we interact with others and respond to situations.

NLP (Neuro-Linguistic Programming) has 16 presuppositions - basic principles that guide the way you act. They provide a foundation for effectiveness. Here we share a few that we have wrapped our own bow around, that have proved really valuable to us. By acting in accord with these principles it helps you RESPOND rather than REACT in difficult situations.

- **Everything is true from a certain perspective**
- **Behind every action is a positive intention**
- **Those with the greatest flexibility have the greatest choices**
- **People are not difficult, they are just different**

Can you think of a time when you didn't act in accord with these principles, what was the impact of your actions?

Now think about how things might have played out if you did uphold these basic principles - how would the outcome have been different?

Becoming a Learning Entrepreneur

In today's climate, organisations need to be fluid and that means your learning and development function needs to be highly flexible too. You may find your team are taking on new responsibilities or are being asked to respond to requests with greater speed and with new, more cost effective solutions.

Today's world of work is increasingly complex and information rich. But this information is not so easy to decipher its value or meaning. This means that today's learning professionals are not just deliverers of learning but increasingly you need to be trusted partners who can help managers and staff alike navigate through diverse options and support a continued development in everyone, all the time. You are not just providers but also...

- curators
- maximisers
- guides
- champions
- challengers.

You face a fluid backdrop and need to be commercially flexible to ensure that every contribution is valid and valued at all levels within the organisation.

You need to be able to help yourself and others to make connections and deepen relationships even when it is not possible to do this face to face in the office. It's a whole new skill set to explore.

Your organisation needs Learning Entrepreneurs.

Learning Entrepreneurs recognise and seize opportunities to innovate. They develop great partnerships with their customers based on a sound understanding of commercial needs. They are prepared to challenge the status quo and accept the risks involved with taking action. A Learning Entrepreneur is someone with passion who sees opportunities, then generates innovative, creative ideas to effect a change.

Learning Entrepreneurs are commercially creative and always have an eye on the value they offer.

Action

Take a look at the behaviour wheel below and take a few moments to identify your strengths and opportunities for stretch. There are four core areas, each of which have three behaviours that define them. For each behaviour identify what mark out of 10 you would give yourself. If you're bold you might even ask some of your colleagues to mark you too! Add this to the next page and think about some ideas you can implement to provide additional focus and drive.

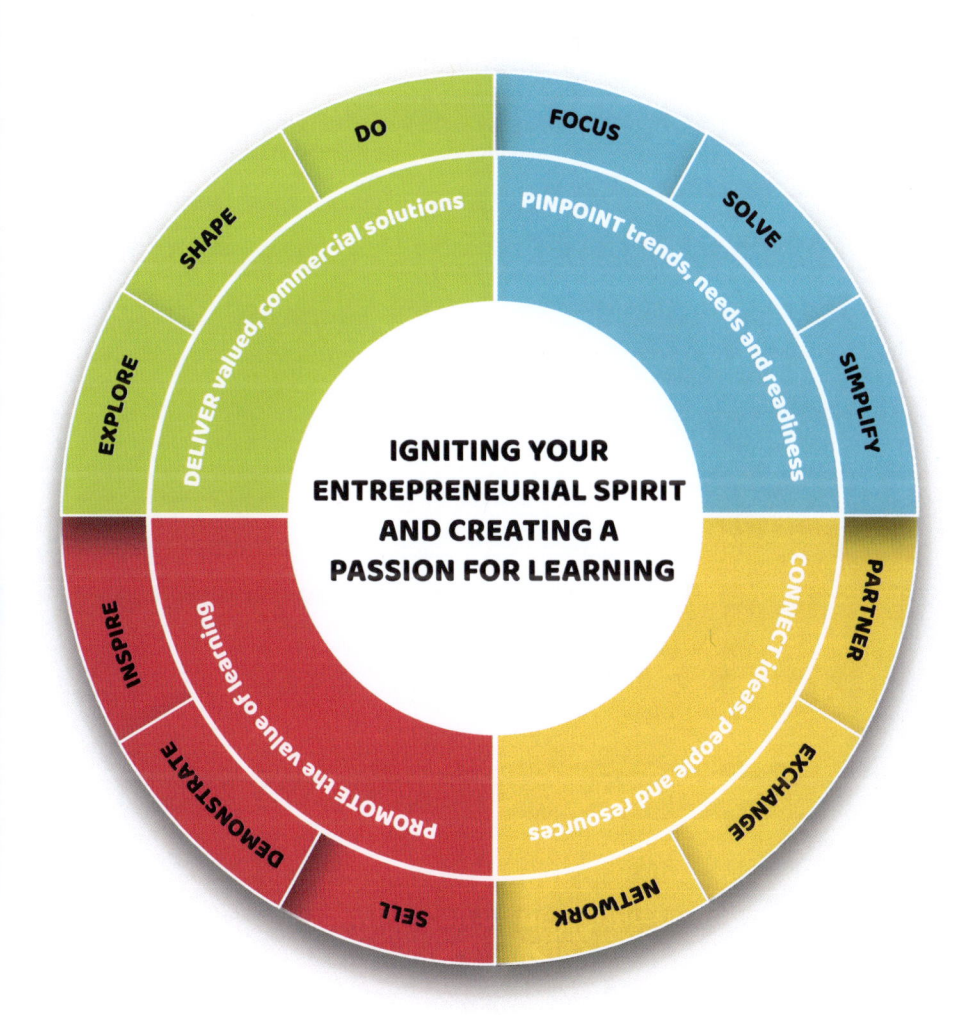

IGNITING YOUR ENTREPRENEURIAL SPIRIT AND CREATING A PASSION FOR LEARNING

- DO / SHAPE / EXPLORE — DELIVER valued, commercial solutions
- FOCUS / SOLVE / SIMPLIFY — PINPOINT trends, needs and readiness
- PARTNER / EXCHANGE / NETWORK — CONNECT ideas, people and resources
- INSPIRE / DEMONSTRATE / SELL — PROMOTE the value of learning

Your action plan

		Score/ 10
PINPOINT Enables you to harness your own resourcefulness to solve the problems that matter to the business. These behaviours ensure you focus on the right things, filter out distracting noise and pinpoint what will really make a difference.	**FOCUS:** How familiar are you with the organisational strategy? How well does learning contribute to the challenges the organisation faces?	
	SOLVE: How well do your solutions really solve organisational challenges and get people fit for the future?	
	SIMPLIFY: Is learning simple and easy to access? Can you respond to the changing needs of the organisation?	

Overall score /30
Ideas for action

		Score/10
CONNECT Recognises that learning doesn't exist in a vacuum; working collaboratively with all areas of your business enables really great learning solutions to take shape. These behaviours ensure you connect ideas, information and people in a way that creates powerful sustainable partnerships.	**PARTNER:** Are you a trusted partner in the business? Do you have a seat at the table or are you the last to be brought into any discussions?	
	EXCHANGE: Are you a go-to person for advice and ideas?	
	NETWORK: How effective is your network inside and outside the organisation to help you develop ideas and create value?	

Overall score /30
Ideas for action

		Score/ 10
PROMOTE Is about speaking to the business about learning in a way that generates momentum, gains traction and delivers results. These behaviours ensure that you grab attention and create an insatiable passion for learning across the whole organisation.	**SELL:** How well do you gain support for learning around the organisation based on the functional, economic and emotional needs of your stakeholders?	
	DEMONSTRATE: How effective a role model are you for continuous learning and being curious and flexible?	
	INSPIRE: What levels of engagement for learning do you have? How can you improve this through inspiring people to act?	

Overall score /30
Ideas for action

		Score/ 10
DELIVER Enables you to create learning solutions that generate a buzz and excitement around the organisation that can't be ignored! These behaviours ensure your solutions deliver real, commercial improvements.	**EXPLORE:** How well do you research your ideas both with stakeholders, users and outside the organisation?	
	SHAPE: Are you agile and responsive? How quickly can you get to a solution that gains traction and delivers real value?	
	DO: How action-orientated are you? Do you see the big picture or do you have a tendency to get stuck in the detail?	

Overall score /30
Ideas for action

Quick reflection

PINPOINT
What business problems have your learning solutions solved in the last 6 months?

CONNECT
How well are you capitalising on your networks?

PROMOTE
When did a customer last say 'WOW' in response to your learning solutions? When did you last influence a Board level decision?

DELIVER
What is the most courageous or innovative thing you have done in the last year?

Supercharge your credibility

"It's not what you say it's the way that you DO it!"
Your credibility is at the heart of your impact and will determine whether people buy-in to your ideas or not. So try out these top tips to help you reinforce your gravitas, now.

Actively raise your game
Look for opportunities where you can raise your game.
- Think of the people and projects that will challenge you and keep your finger on the pulse of current and future business needs.
- Which colleagues could you benefit from working alongside?
- Which client groups have you yet to work with?
- Where would you need to adjust your approach in order to deliver learning successfully?

Be Bold
Be brave and do something revolutionary and different. Use this book to help you really plan out how you can transform your learning to be world class.

Assess current and future needs of the organisation
Talk with your senior team to get crystal clear about what the current, and just as important, future business needs are. Also discuss with them what type of learning strategy needs to be in place to meet those needs. Really prepare the questions you want to ask to probe and strengthen your understanding. Be prepared to challenge perceptions and ideas.

Research
Undertake research to investigate the latest trends in learning. Assess what latest learning methods you can incorporate into your L&D strategy to meet current and future business needs. Whenever you hear about what other companies are doing divide the information into two:
1. What's good about this that I can do something with right now and how?
2. What's good about this that I need to work on for the future?
You'll notice that we've urged you not to critique this information but to seek out the good stuff. By doing this you'll leave your mind more open to accept ideas rather than dismiss them.

Great consultants ask...

...great questions and are not afraid to really hear the answer and probe.

Draw up a list of questions you could ask your 'client' who has requested a learning solution. This list must include at least 3 unusual and thought provoking questions. Here are some examples to get you started:

- If you had no resource limitations what would you do?
- If we could change just one thing about the way your team behaved what would that be?
- What would be the impact if this training didn't take place?

Key takeaways

1. As an L&D professional you are a role model for others - use it wisely.

2. Always consider what VALUE you are adding from your customers' perspective.

3. Don't let your fear stop you making progress. Use these 3 steps to help you overcome your hesitancy:
   1. Let go of limiting beliefs
   2. Learn from others
   3. Mitigate your risks

4. Adopting a Dotcom mindset will help you elevate your thinking and your value.

5. Explore your beliefs about others to ensure these aren't holding you back. This will help you RESPOND rather than having a knee jerk reaction.

6. The role of the L&D professional is getting increasingly complex. No longer are you just providers but now you are curators, maximisers, guides, champions and challengers.

7. Focus on becoming a Learning Entrepreneur. Learning Entrepreneurs are commercially creative and always have an eye on the value they offer.

8. "It's not what you say, it's the way that you DO it". Get commercial, know the organisational strategy and be clear about how learning contributes to it.

> **Success is not final. Failure is not fatal: It is the courage to continue that counts.**
> Winston Churchill

Before we move on...

Take a few moments to jot down the thoughts, ideas or actions that have come to you from exploring this section.

PART THREE
MOVING TOWARDS A LEARNING ORGANISATION

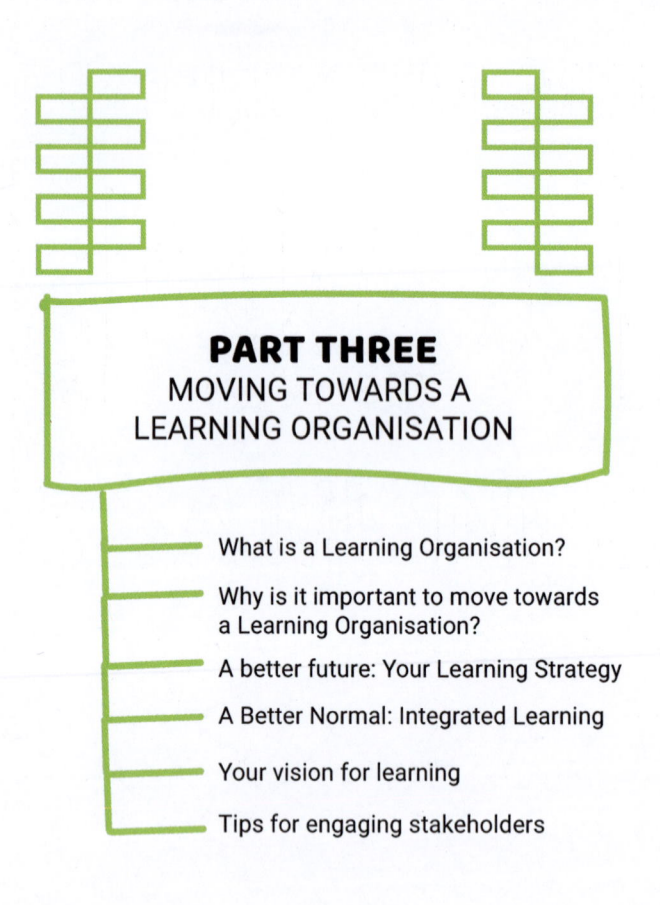

- What is a Learning Organisation?
- Why is it important to move towards a Learning Organisation?
- A better future: Your Learning Strategy
- A Better Normal: Integrated Learning
- Your vision for learning
- Tips for engaging stakeholders

What is a Learning Organisation?

"A learning organisation is an organisation skilled at creating, acquiring, and transferring knowledge, and at modifying its behaviour to reflect new knowledge and insights."
Harvard Business Review

In essence this is about freeing people up and actively encouraging a spirit of collaboration and supportive exploration of ideas. In today's crazy world, the old system of knowledge acquisition simply does not work any more. It is the collective thinking and iterations that collaboration enables that ignites the spark of great ideas. This is where learning comes in. Your learning strategy needs to enable this to take shape. Your approach can create the supportive culture and provide the essential skills for people to perform in this environment.

Why is it important to move towards a Learning Organisation?

Let's start by recognising just how crucial learning is in helping your organisation thrive.

Traditional learning simply does not keep up with the pace of our working world.

It's time to change. The argument has been made for resources not courses for many years. But thinking about the engagement and user experience is key. It's not enough to just provide a catalogue of materials for people to access. That works for people who are confident and motivated to learn. But for many in organisations this is not the case. Most people need more support, guidance and challenge to help them process the learning. It's important to shift your emphasis to 'how can I help them get the right things done?'

It's important to think about your capabilities as a Learning Organisation and ensuring that learning is seen as a thread to help the organisation thrive. This means engagement at all levels.

Think:
1. How can I relate learning to the organisation's goals?
2. How do I engage leaders so they want to be involved?
3. How can I encourage managers to help their teams continuously reflect and learn?

What do you want your learning environment to be like?
e.g. Resources, psychological safety, valuing difference, openness to new ideas, reflective practices, building in challenge

How do Leaders need to behave to demonstrate commitment?
e.g. Learning role models, supportive, transformational in their approach to work

How will your learning processes and practices engage and excite?
e.g. Experimentation and challenge, style, data provided, targetting, analysis, collaboration, goal setting

What do you want your learning environment to be like?

How do you need Leaders to behave to demonstrate commitment to learning?

How will your learning processes and practices engage and excite?

Remember to enter into the debate on our Facebook group/ Learning Entrepreneurs to explore this further.

BUT ...
Let's get real ...

It's not that simple now is it?

A better future: Your learning strategy

Organisations flipped to remote working overnight.

Many of these are seeing positive benefits to critical measures like reduction in expenses, increased productivity and engagement. It is also increasingly popular with staff, many of whom would like to see the opportunity of some kind of remote working to be available to them in the future too. But it's not without its challenges.

Distance, different communication methods, intensity of screen presence and organisational culture may act as barriers to ongoing learning and can be debilitating if not addressed.

Enhancing your learning culture will help to mitigate some of the challenges and can be instrumental in connecting people to:

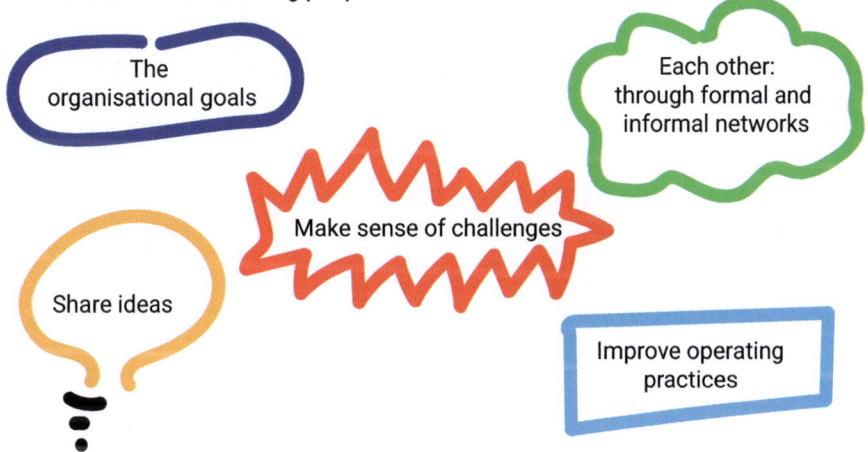

- The organisational goals
- Each other: through formal and informal networks
- Make sense of challenges
- Share ideas
- Improve operating practices

In the not too distant future successful organisations must at some point face the possibility of not returning to full office based work. Many will still have a remote workforce, either full or partial. Their staff will need access to learning that not only improves their technical skills but also the enhanced core skills needed to help move both the organisation and their own careers forward in this 'better normal'. For the immediate future it is unlikely that effective classroom training will be a feasible option.

This is where a strategically deployed digital learning platform supports the organisation. Many organisations have already made the move to virtual learning - they've had to. But there is so much more to it than simply deploying an LMS and hoping for the best. The best organisations are building a vibrant community hub and considering the user experience to ensure rich, engaging resources with challenges to help everyone thrive. This is the next generation learning platform - a social learning platform

Instant reaction

When you think about your organisation, its capability to thrive against the challenges ahead and your learning strategy to support this, what score out of 10 would you give it?

① ② ③ ④ ⑤ ⑥ ⑦ ⑧ ⑨ ⑩

Why did you give it that score?

→

Let's start to explore what a great learning strategy might look like to help you move towards a Learning Organisation.

A better normal: Integrated Learning

Just as organisations had to transfer to remote working overnight, so learning needs to embrace the opportunity to integrate digital learning to equip its people with the tools to collaborate, share, upskill and explore together.

- A well-deployed, social learning platform supports the development of people's critical skills in line with the business strategy.

- Not only that, it also enhances the organisation's culture and enables people to live the values in their day to day work.

- It enables you to be agile to respond to the rapidly changing landscape; to pilot and experiment.

- It enables you to create learning journeys that integrate all opportunities available including user generated content, short classes (virtually or if appropriate face to face), job guides, how to's, challenges, curiosity builders, self-reflection, on job coaching, buddying and mentoring.

- And finally, it provides learning at point of need by enabling users to easily search for what they need, when they need it.

If you don't start to integrate digital learning now into your strategy, you are in danger of quickly becoming extinct and your organisation will not be able to equip its people with the skills needed to thrive.

So, in preparing your learning strategy you will find 4 key considerations on the next page for you to think about.

Go beyond
The best integrated learning platforms are so much more than an LMS. They create a space for communication and learning within relevant communities so that everyone has access to opportunities to help them achieve results and fulfil their potential. For an organisation it will also provide a high powered back end that provides critical data to help you effectively target what you need, when you need it and in a way that resonates.

Organisation wide
This cannot be a top down initiative; it needs to involve every level across all functions. And with remote working so prevalent it also needs to avoid being head office centric. 'Global' and 'local' need to work together to ensure the learning lands. Engagement and resources developed across all functions will make it more relevant and valuable. Finally, and most importantly, your managers need to set an example. They are essential in supporting the development of their teams and leading the way as you enhance your learning culture. Working in partnership with your managers, you can ensure your organisation is fit for the future. Together you can remove barriers, set the tone and guide people to access what is relevant for them.

Integration
A great digital platform strives to help overwhelmed and busy people improve their performance where and when it matters with the very best, carefully selected experiences and resources available. It is not just a matter of reloading everything you have available in one place and hoping for the best. Your learning strategy needs to embrace all that is good, not just switch from in person to digital. It demands you really think about what is needed and how best to provide it using all the tools available to you.

Be clear on what you are measuring
In agile organisations with networked teams, rapid decision making and learning cycles, the human capital of your organisation needs to be empowered to adapt and learn quickly. As such, they need guidance on what great looks like. Whilst many organisations adopt a competency framework to guide this thinking, often this can be cumbersome and inaccessible for people. As such, a keen spotlight on critical skills helps consolidate the focus on the skills and behaviours that drive success. These critical skills can then easily be benchmarked and measured, guiding action and setting a positive tone of high expectation. Using digital analytics can equip learning functions with the ability to understand and evaluate business impact and adjust their approaches quickly to add greater value.

Some questions to inspire your learning strategy

	Now	Future
How much support does learning have from key stakeholders?		
Where do people go now to get their information and how effective is this method?		
How does learning help people do a better job?		
How do you help people share their expertise, ideas, workarounds etc quickly so everyone can learn fast?		
How do you know that learning is making an impact where it needs to and adapt where it's needed?		
How effectively do you cascade critical messages, fast? And how do you measure their impact?		
What is your user experience like now to encourage engagement and collaboration?		
How do you measure business impact?		

What other questions would you add to help you shape your strategy?

Asking questions is a great way to shape your thinking. What questions have you got that you'd like to ask our Facebook group?

Your vision for learning

Now you've explored ideas for an integrated strategy. What will make YOUR learning strategy a 10/10 to help create a BETTER normal?

Your vision

① ② ③

Moving towards your vision can feel like a HUGE leap but if you break it down, what are your first 3 steps to getting there? **WHAT ACTIONS WILL YOU TAKE?**

Did you think about.....

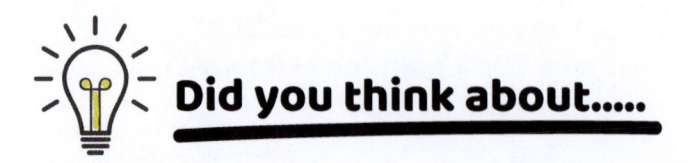

YOUR WHY?
What's your purpose in your 10/10? When you have a compelling purpose it's easier to focus your mind on achieving it. AND it is also clearer for everyone to buy into.

Your WHO?
Who in your organisation is going to help you achieve your goals? Who will be your champions or early adopters? Who will give you time, money and resources to help?

Your HOW?
How will you convince them that this is the right way to progress. What's In It For Them to help you?

Your METRICS?
What metrics can you develop that will help convince people that this is the right way to progress? What data will help you show when your vision is a success?

Your STORY?
Facts and figures are only a small part of your business case. Stories move people through their emotion and imagination... "Imagine a world where people..." is a great way to start.

What challenges will you have to overcome to make your learning strategy a 10/10?

Take a few moments and jot these down below.
Take no more than 3 minutes to consider what your immediate challenges might be. Feel free to write or draw etc. Set a timer... remember no more than 3 minutes!

The more you prepare yourself for the challenges ahead the better equipped you will be to handle them. So let's dig a little deeper on the next page.

Your stakeholders hold the key

Your stakeholders are such a crucial piece of your jigsaw for making great things happen, you can't afford to leave their support to chance. They hold the key for helping you overcome many of your challenges.

Tips for engaging stakeholders

1. Identify and map your stakeholders

High ↑ How much power do they hold?	Keep Satisfied	Engage & collaborate
	Monitor	Keep Informed
	Low How interested are they? **High** →	

2. Determine their business priorities
- What do they care about?
- What are their business objectives?

3. WIIFT
Tap into their personal priorities: motivations/drivers

4. Determine how your main objectives support the business
Keep laser focused on them.

5. Communicate the VALUE

6. Be clear on risks
Likelihood ✗ Severity

"The essence of teaching is to make learning CONTAGIOUS, to make one idea spark another"

Key takeaways

1. A Learning Organisation is skilled at creating, transferring and acquiring knowledge and shifting behaviour as a result.

2. Leaders are crucial in affecting a change in behaviour.

3. Organisations have had to flip overnight. How well has your learning strategy supported this transformation?

4. An LMS will help you 'push' knowledge but a social learning platform will enable you to engage, exchange and build learning and ideas.

5. Take time to plan your vision for learning so that it is not just right for now but will help you future proof your organisation.

6. Communicate, not just in terms of facts and figures, but also paint the picture and build a positive story of possibility.

7. Anticipate your challenges - being forearmed gives you strength

8. People remember difference not sameness - make people think by offering a variety of ideas.

9. Ask great questions of yourself AND of others.

> **People are social beings and want interaction. Social learning is the primary form of learning, just as word of mouth advertising is the highest form of advertising.**
> Stephen Covey

Before we move on...

Take a few moments to jot down the thoughts, ideas or actions that have come to you from exploring this section.

PART FOUR
ENGAGING LEARNERS

- Creating an engaging user experience
- Principle 1: Follow the full Learning Cycle
- Principle 2: Get into the Learning Zone
- Principle 3: Keep it SAVI
- Principle 4: Promote Discovery
- Principle 5: Mirror Real Life
- Principle 6: Set Up, Stand Back, Pull Together
- Principle 7: Layer Learning
- Principle 8: Offer learning through CPR

So you've taken the plunge

You are integrating digital as part of your learning strategy

It could be pretty straightforward to make the conversion - you can shoot some videos, maybe animate a few, create more e-learning resources and slide decks. But it is also an opportunity for you to challenge the way you create your user experience. Whether you are creating webinars, videos, pdfs etc, THINK...

PEOPLE REMEMBER DIFFERENCE NOT SAMENESS

Let's explore what that might be like.

Creating an engaging user experience

In our haste it is easy to look for the quick, simple solution. Many people opt for a curated content library and think volume matters.

But before you rush out and grab yourself one of these, stop and think.

People are inundated with information all the time. They simply have access to too much and can often feel overwhelmed which can put the kibosh on any good intentions you had.

Planning what people need and want will really help ensure you deliver the right solution for them and your organisation.

Quantity does not equal quality.

Your people are the source of your knowledge. They have worked out how to do things swiftly and simply over time. Peer to peer learning has great power, if managed carefully, and this is where your platform comes in. Through a digital platform you can provide dynamic 'how to' resources from the horse's mouth and support this with collaboration, on-job coaching, buddying etc. This can be supplemented with carefully curated content from public sources. And for more technical/regulatory learning, internally produced materials provide a great balance of resources.

This is NOT about throwing the baby out with the bathwater. As an industry there is a tendency to be drawn to the 'new shiny toy'. In fact there is a syndrome for it! When people were dissatisfied with the outcomes from classroom learning, rather than exploring what the inadequacies were and dealing with these, learning professionals reacted by moving everything they could to e-learning. When dissatisfied with this they moved to an LMS and so on. There are brilliant best practice examples for all of these and we need to embrace all of the incredible, diverse opportunities to now help people grow and ensure our organisations thrive. This is about offering diverse solutions to drive learning. It is about integrating the best of everything in one, easy to access platform with smart analytics to help you target your effort in an agile manner.

Whatever you do remember this:

1. The user experience is critical.
If finding the right materials quickly is tough or they are faced with dozens of sources with little differentiation then user engagement will fall off a cliff. You need to create resources that inspire, peak curiosity and encourage engagement. You want your people to think, challenge, reflect and respond. You want a movement of learners who are inspired to continually learn.

2. People remember difference, not sameness.
In today's fast paced world where we need information and we need it now, it can be hard to distinguish between what is important and what is just interesting. Help people process learning by offering up challenges or questions to make them think. And ensure that learning is served in different ways to appeal to what is unique in individuals.

So let's move on to look at what great learning looks like in this new world.

Think for a moment where you get your best learning from.

Ask a few people where they get theirs from and do some research to see what's out there. Jot down in the box some of these you'd like to leverage in this brave new world.

People are different

They are as diverse in their needs as there are sources of information and ideas out there in the world. You cannot hope to sheep dip people and think you've ticked the box before you move onto the next thing.

Creating a resource library is a brilliant tool for people who are motivated and skilled learners. Many people in organisations are not this. They need significantly more support to help them access the right resources to support their development. They need to learn how to learn and you need to help them engage by creating exciting opportunities to entice them. This is where our eight principles of learning come in to help you develop exciting, relevant and poignant learning opportunities for everyone to stretch themselves.

> **People with high assurance in their capabilities approach difficult tasks as challenges to be mastered rather than as threats to be avoided**

Albert Bandura

How does your organisation demonstrate their belief in people's abilities and encourage them to play to their strengths?

Principle 1:
Follow the full LEARNING CYCLE

PRINCIPLE 1:
Applying the LEARNING CYCLE

Help learners maximise the potential of any learning; whether face to face, online or social by:

1. **Preparation:** Building excitement, curiosity and WIIFM (What's in it for me) for what is about to come
2. **Presentation:** Making new information interesting and stimulating; not just a list of facts.
3. **Practice:** Helping learners develop comfort and confidence in new ideas by setting challenges to integrate ideas into their day to day routine.
4. **Performance:** Helping them directly apply learning and receive feedback on what to continually develop.

4 Performance — APPLYING LEARNING & CONTINUING TO DEVELOP

1 Preparation — BUILDING EXCITEMENT & RAISING CURIOSITY

3 Practice — GAINING CONFIDENCE & COMFORT

2 Presentation — DISCOVERING NEW INFORMATION AND IDEAS

Devised by the superstar that is David Meier

Applying the LEARNING CYCLE

WHAT % OF YOUR TIME IS FOCUSED ON EACH QUADRANT?

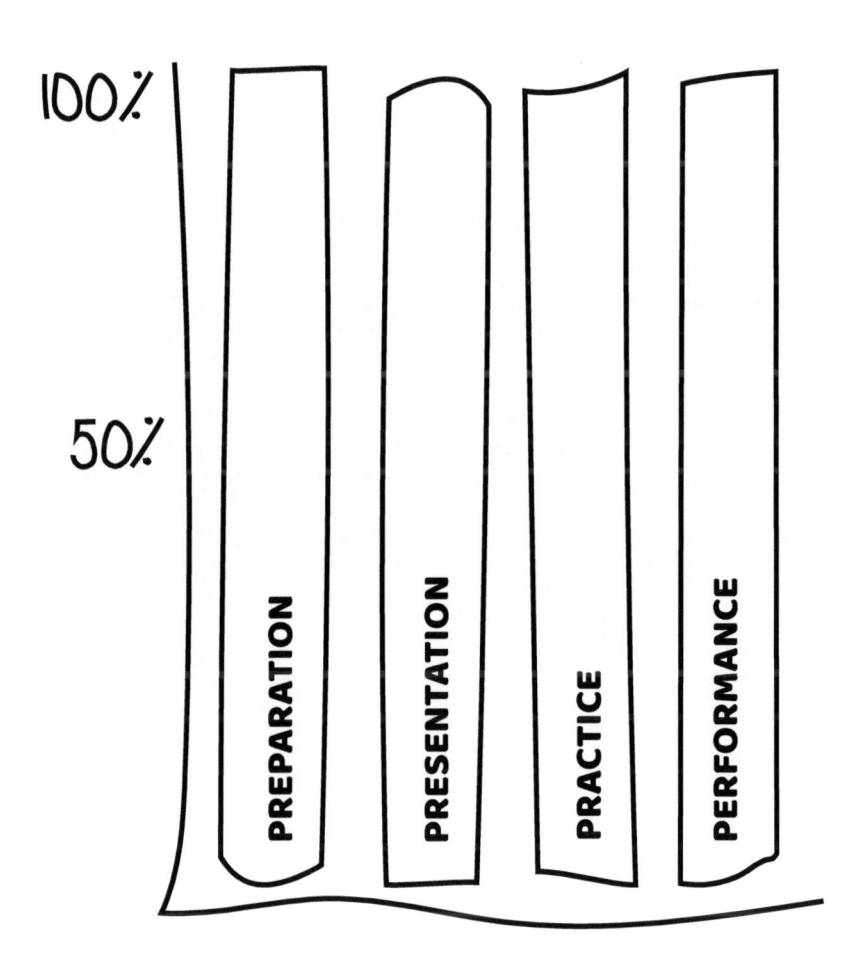

100%

50%

PREPARATION

PRESENTATION

PRACTICE

PERFORMANCE

PREPARATION: Your ideas for building curiosity, interest and excitement	**PRESENTATION:** Your ideas to help learners discover for themselves
PRACTICE: Your ideas to help learners practice safely	**PERFORMANCE:** Your ideas for ensuring learners go away and apply learning

PRINCIPLE 2: Get into the LEARNING ZONE

People learn more and remember more when they are in a good physical, mental and emotional state. We can help them achieve this by keeping them mentally challenged, physically active and encouraging an emotional connection to what they are learning

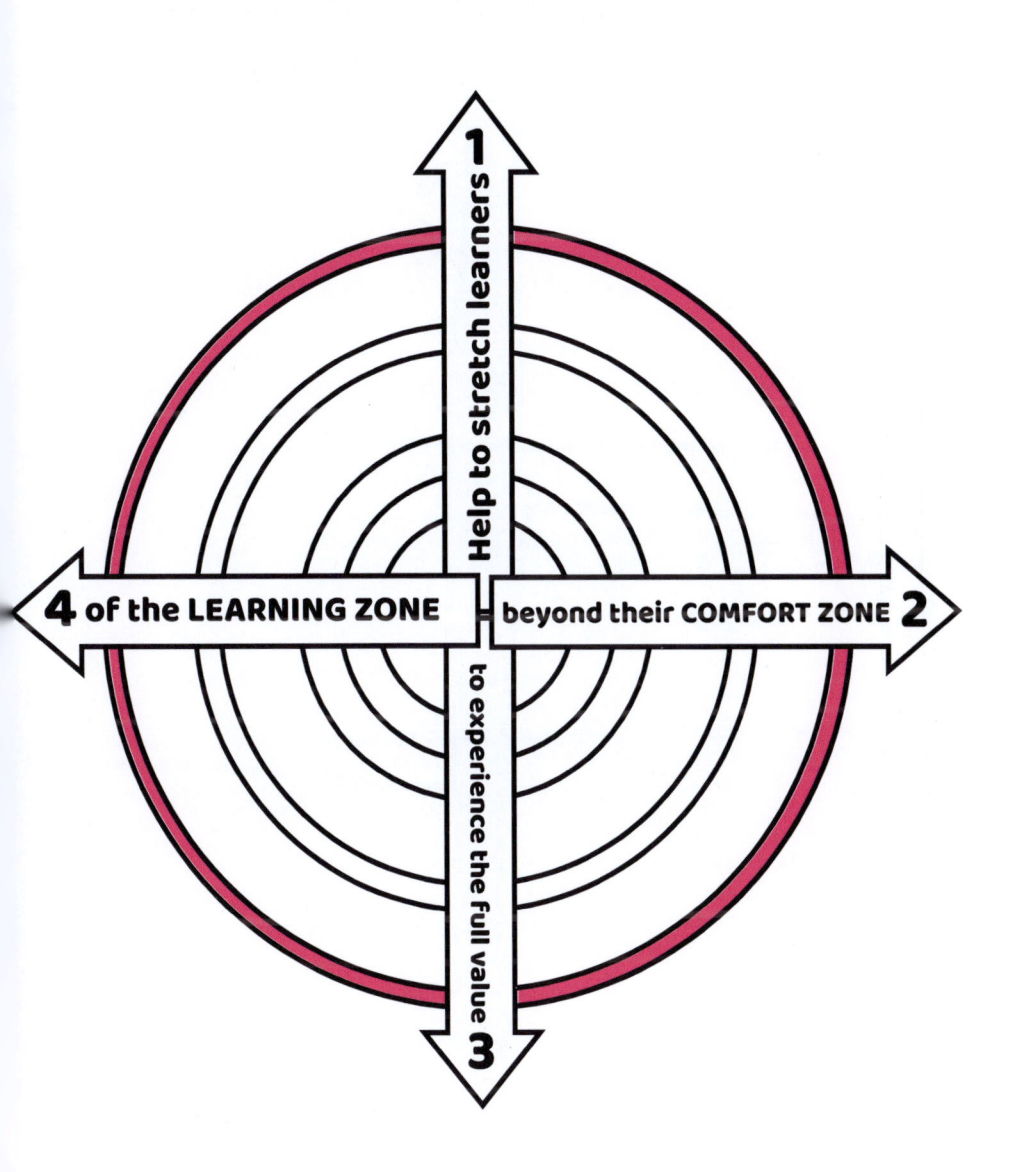

1 Help to stretch learners

2 beyond their COMFORT ZONE

3 to experience the full value

4 of the LEARNING ZONE

What additional ideas do you have?

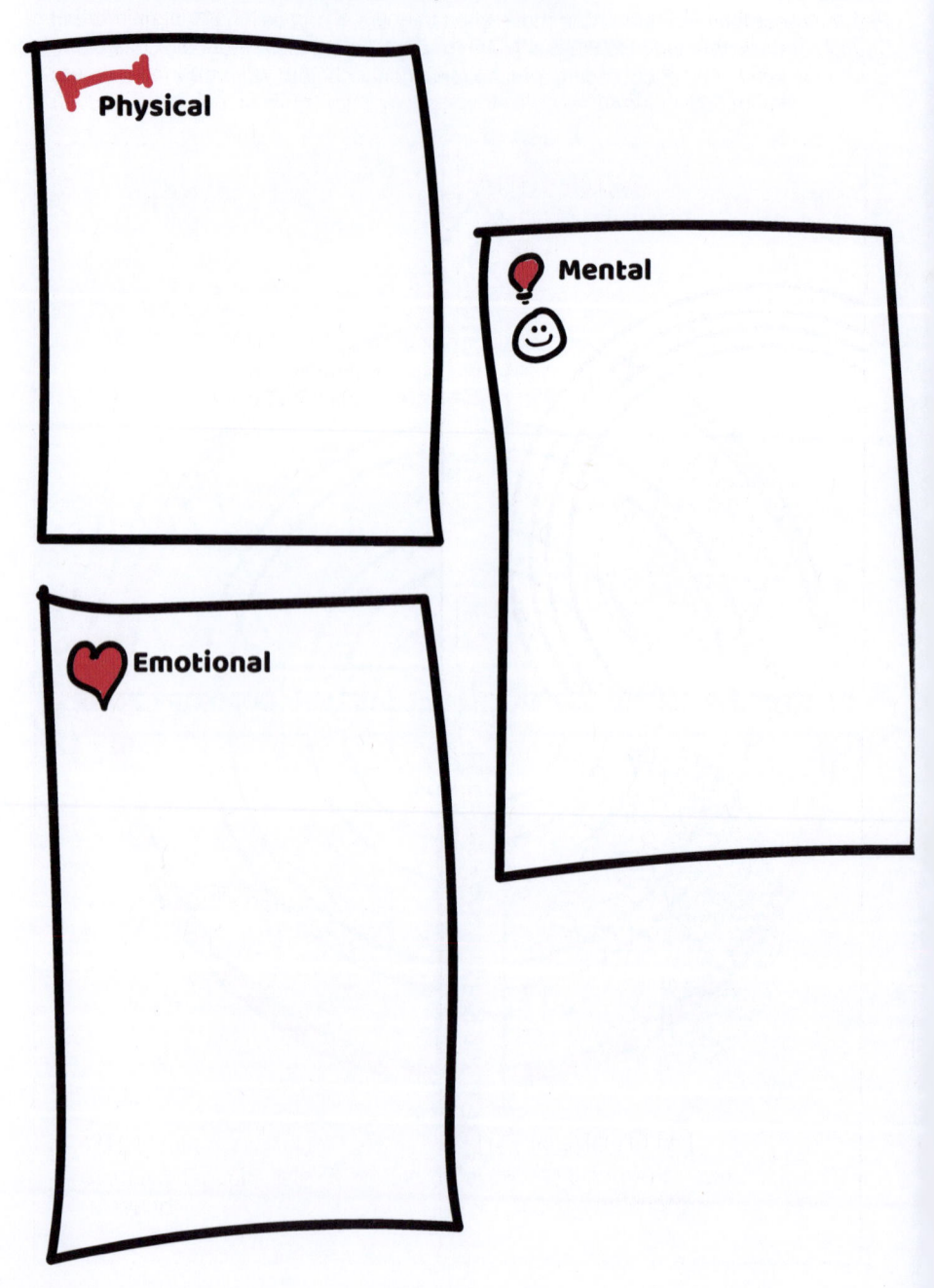

Physical

Mental

Emotional

> **Live as if you were to die tomorrow. LEARN as if you were to live forever.**
> Ghandi

What does this look like for you?

Principle 3: Keep it SAVI

David Meier simplified learning styles theories into these four critical elements. You need to help learners to learn through moving & doing, talking & listening, seeing & picturing, at the same time! This caters for individual preference as well as making stronger memories. To turn these memories into real learning you need to add reflection & problem solving so people can and will do something as a result.

SOMATIC
Learning through moving & doing

AUDITORY
Learning through talking & listening

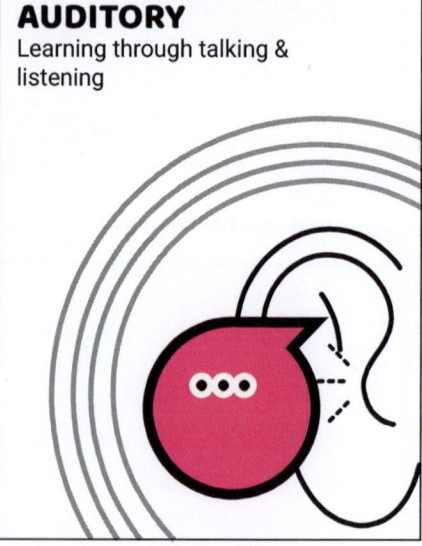

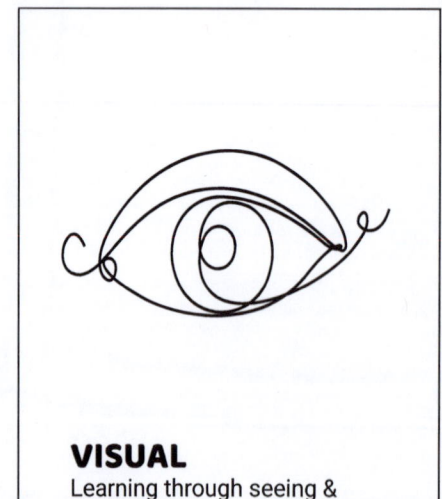

VISUAL
Learning through seeing & picturing

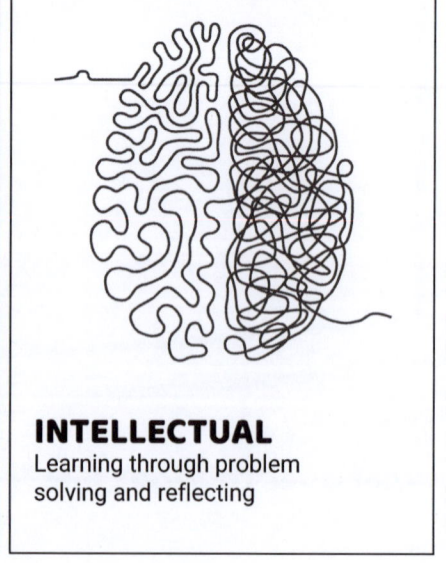

INTELLECTUAL
Learning through problem solving and reflecting

Keep Learning SAVI

ON A SCALE OF 1 - 10
HOW SAVI IS YOUR LEARNING RIGHT NOW?

① ② ③ ④ ⑤ ⑥ ⑦ ⑧ ⑨ ⑩

It's all change in learning isn't it? And many people are experiencing the good, the bad and the ugly of learning. Thinking of SAVI, jot down some ideas of how you can bring your learning to life using this principle. Think about the opportunities you are providing right now including digital resources or virtual classrooms if relevant.

"**Education** is the most powerful weapon which you can use to change the **world**."
Nelson Mandela

Principle 4: Promote DISCOVERY

People learn more when they discover it for themselves rather than being spoon-fed answers. And when they have found their own answers they are more likely to put these into practice.

Take a fresh look at some of your recent learning designs.
What do you PRESENT when you could be *promoting discovery?* What improvements can you now make?

LEARNING IS A TREASURE

that will follow its owner everywhere

Chinese Proverb

Organisations are under tremendous pressure. How will you ensure that your learning can be designed rapidly, be fit for helping people adapt and be engaging all at the same time? Now more than ever learning is a foundation to help your organisation thrive.

Principle 5: Mirror Real Life

People need to be able to relate what they are learning to their own life, work and experience. Otherwise they might learn some great new information or skills but not know how to use them in the real world.

So if your learners.....

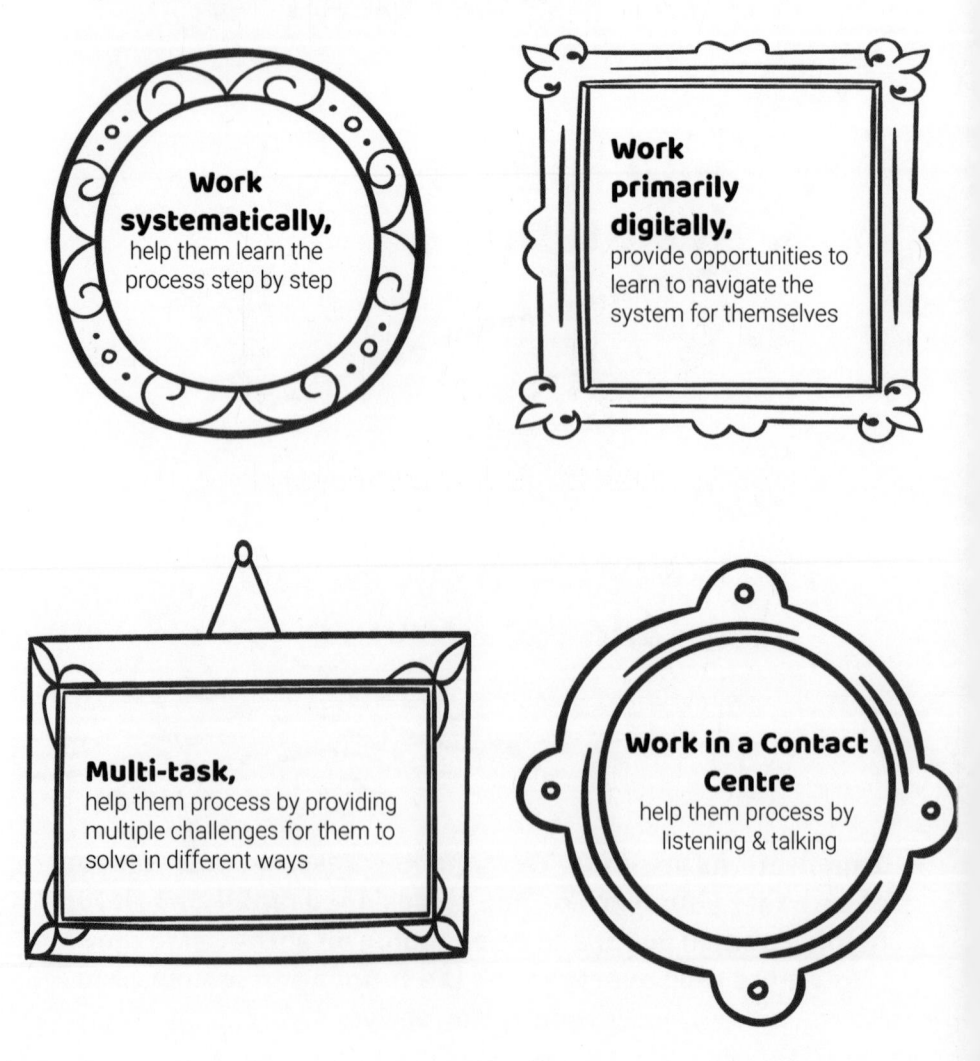

Work systematically, help them learn the process step by step

Work primarily digitally, provide opportunities to learn to navigate the system for themselves

Multi-task, help them process by providing multiple challenges for them to solve in different ways

Work in a Contact Centre help them process by listening & talking

How can you amplify the value of learning and mirror real life for your learners by using the context in which they are working?

"GENIUS is INITIATIVE on *fire*"

Holbrook Jackson

Principle 6: Set Up, Stand Back, Pull Together

Whether you are offering virtual classrooms, face to face or digital content you are facilitating learning.

Great facilitators make sure learners are clear about the purpose and output, and then get out of the way while they learn. Facilitators then need to step in again to help learners make sense of what they have discovered so they can take action as a result.

What can you do or say to make your set up of learning INSPIRING?

What examples of great review questions can you ask to pull it all TOGETHER?

"I am not afraid of storms for I am **LEARNING** to sail my ship."
Louisa M. Alcott

Principle 7: Layer Learning

We learn through repetition.
The more often we encounter new information and practice new skills, the better we get. It works best to start simply and build in complexity. Remember the brain is a multi-processor. It is stimulated by challenge so don't spoon-feed it.

Think About....

How can you scaffold learning starting with the simplest thing they need to know?

What different ways can you encourage learners to view the situation?

Think... conceptually, practically, from the customer perspective, from the organisation's angle or what about from the manager's viewpoint?

How can you make a story map visually piecing all the information together?

Think about the outcome you want to achieve and work back from there.

We often try to simplify information to make it easier for people to pick up but ... Think about your group, how can you present the information so it's intellectually stimulating for them?

What team problem can you give the group to solve? Think about giving different members unique information that they need to piece together. You can always use a red herring too!

> **Never become so much of an** expert that you stop gaining expertise. **View life as a** continuous learning experience.
> **Denis Waitley**

Principle 8: Offer learning through C.P.R.

Not all learning in real life happens through 'reading the manual'.
Instead we often just plunge in and go for it. Our own reaction to experiences also provide great learning if we are encouraged to stop to think about it. We can replicate this in our learning by sharing information (Content), creating experiences (Process) and helping people learn from their own reactions. (Reaction)

Content:
Great questions to review content

Process:
Great questions to explore what they have learnt through their experience

Reaction:
Great questions to review their feelings about the learning

Key takeaways

1. Your user experience (learner experience) is much more than just providing learning for them to consume. Engagement is critical to ensuring a great offer that people want to use.

2. Any piece of learning you provide needs four steps:
   - Draw people to it,
   - Offer insight/ideas in the moment of need,
   - Provide challenge to help them process these ideas, and finally
   - Help them understand what success will look like for them so they can benchmark their performance.

3. It doesn't need to be complicated. In fact the simpler the better.

4. Remember that people learn differently so aim to incorporate SAVI into all that you provide.

5. People don't just learn solely from the CONTENT you provide, they also learn through the way in which you serve up the learning (your PROCESS). And remember to help them learn from their REACTIONS (good and bad).

6. Quantity does not equal quality. Make sure that you provide what is needed and make it easy to access.

> **The wisest mind has something yet to learn.**

George Santayanos

Before we move on...

Take a few moments to jot down the thoughts, ideas or actions that have come to you from exploring this section.

PART FIVE
PULLING IT ALL TOGETHER

- Time for action
- Challenge Time
- Go for it! Your commitments
- Enjoy your success

Time for action

Congratulations! You've done a lot of work to get this far.
It shows how important this is to you to stretch yourself. You've developed your thinking and probably done your own research along the way. Hopefully you have also engaged with the Facebook group and gained some new friends and valuable ideas. So what do you do next?

It's time for **ACTION!**

Many people have ideas, dreams and ambitions that they never pursue. For some, fear of failure holds them back, for others it's the fear of the unknown. You might be one of those people who seek perfection. But if you've made it this far you owe it to yourself to take that action.

Challenge Time

On page 40 you scored your learning strategy a ____

3 TO THRIVE
Tony Robbins encourages us to take 3 actions a day that will help us make progress. So what 3 actions will you take TODAY to improve your score?

①

②

③

Share your ideas, experience and insights with a like-minded community who are exploring similar challenges to you

SIGN UP
To our Facebook group to deepen your understanding, share ideas and strengthen your focus. facebook.com/groups/learningentrepreneurs

Dream BIG

MAKE IT
To help you keep an eye on your vision (even when the going gets tough) take 15 minutes and make a collage or draw a picture that shows you what positive impact your learning will have on results and people. Really think about what you will see, hear and feel around your organisation when you are successful. Post it somewhere you can see it easily to help keep it firmly in mind.

Making it count

It's over to you time. Time to make it count. But before you do, have a think about these final thoughts.

1. You need to feel comfortable with feeling uncomfortable.
Times are changing so rapidly. Our world has been turned on its head and it can be scarey. But it doesn't need to be that way. We talk about helping our learners get into the learning zone and we need to be there too. If we are not feeling uncomfortable then frankly we are doing something wrong; we are overrelying on the way we have done things in the past and with the speed of change in our organisations, we need to lead from the front. Get comfortable with feeling uncomfortable. Do something every day that is stretching you out of your comfort zone. Have that conversation you have been putting off. Connect with someone new on LinkedIn. Comment on an article. Start putting yourself out there and enjoy feeling the stretch.

2. Get comfortable with asking questions - that maybe you don't already know the answer to
To build your credibility in the organisation you need to be able to ask great consulting questions and be open to the answers - even if they are not what you are expecting. By asking great questions you are helping others think, and helping yourself to learn. This has enormous strength. So next time someone asks something of you, stop and ask some questions. By doing this you will get to the nub of what is really needed - it is often not the first thing that is asked for.

3. Be open to innovation and change
A mentor once told us, 'You are only as good as what you do today, not yesterday.' Look for innovative, simple ways of doing things. Seek out continuous improvement in everything you do rather than regurgitating the same old same old. Really challenge yourself to consider the value of every action. Time and attention is poor, so whatever you do has to hit the mark. Make sure you really deliver on what is important to the organisation and help your learners solve their problems in the moment.

4. Don't say no, find alternative solutions
If someone needs help find a way to support them. Know that there is always a way, but sometimes it is easy to say no just because we are overwhelmed. Develop a reputation for being the person who solves problems smartly.

Go for it!

Never before have we faced such immense challenges in Learning and Development and yet, if you are prepared to step up, you CAN make an enormous difference to support your organisation to firstly survive these challenges and then to thrive so that its future is secure.

It really does START WITH YOU.

Learning and Development touches everyone in the organisation. It has the ability to challenge and to heal; to support and explore; to encourage everyone to 'get on the same page' and to collaborate.

By engaging everyone to stretch themselves, be curious and learn, incredible things can happen.

This is your time, make it count!

MY COMMITMENTS

1.

2.

3.

4.

5.

Enjoy your success

Remember success doesn't just happen because you expect it. It is all about your drive and determination.

Here are a few tips to help you.

① Focus on commitment
When the going gets tough, motivation alone will not get you through. Think about how important this is to you and why it's so important. Really clarify your goals and why you want to do this. Shape goals that will help you appreciate the steps you are taking.

② Make the journey fun; not just the end results
Just imagine the fun you can have with making a learning strategy come to life in your organisation. Celebrate each step of the way.

③ Enjoy the discovery
If you focus only on the end result, your enthusiasm will wane quickly. If you focus on the joy of things like discovering new knowledge, connections in ideas and meeting new people this will reinforce your commitment.

④ Manage your state
You know your actions are influenced by your thoughts and emotions. Reflect on your internal dialogue and reframe the message if you need to, to avoid it holding you back. Concentrate on your picture of success to maintain your drive to succeed.

⑤ Plan, prepare and replan
The more you prepare, the better the execution. Really plan how to present yourself and your ideas positively in the eyes of your stakeholders. Remember no communication is neutral - make every conversation count.

"Make your life a masterpiece; imagine no limitation on what you can be, have or do."
Brian Tracy

About the Authors

As founders of Genius Learning, Caroline and Wendy have been at the forefront of innovative learning for the past 25 years. Creating exciting learning solutions for hundreds of global organisations and thousands of people they have carved out a unique reputation for making the complex simple.

Their goal is focused on making work more human and providing learning that reconnects people to the purpose of their work. In doing so helping people see what was previously unnoticed, make new connections with things that were disconnected and giving people a reason to achieve more; to show their EveryDay Genius in work.

They are movers and shakers; learning designers, experience providers; challengers and reflectors and most of all, people lovers.

They are also the people who offer a smile and share their biscuits. They are the first to extend a warm greeting and offer their phone chargers on the train. They have a zest for life and seek out the interesting and fun in the everyday.

"Genius Learning have a unique knack of providing powerful learning experiences in interesting ways that challenge, excite and ignites creative sparks in learners. They are leaders in their field and their purpose shines through in every email, call, session or meeting (virtual or otherwise!)
– they are energisers and they're shakers, they are challengers and cheerleaders and they are people champions and impact creators. If you have a tricky issue to unpick or want to elevate from good to great, I whole heartedly recommend Genius Learning."
James Gilfoyle
Organisational Learning & Development Manager, Edge Hill University

"The team at Genius Learning have always stood out from the crowd. They have a high level of behavioural intelligence and this is something that draws results.
Be it the ability to gauge emotion, to empower, to nurture the ideas in the back of your mind or to support you on a personal or organisational journey. They have this canny way of always finding and adding value. I have been working with them during 2020 and the move from human interaction in my working with them to utilising technology hasn't changed the impact at all. This is testament to the fact that they carry the same degree of energy on and off screen. They are engaging, they know how to mix the technology with their own powerful presentation techniques to keep you focussed throughout. I have found that Genius Learning not only provide the answers to a lot of organisational problems but they have a profound impact on you as the end user or customer and COVID-19 hasn't diluted that."
David Morris
Non-Financial Risk Training and Engagement Specialist, Deutsche Bank

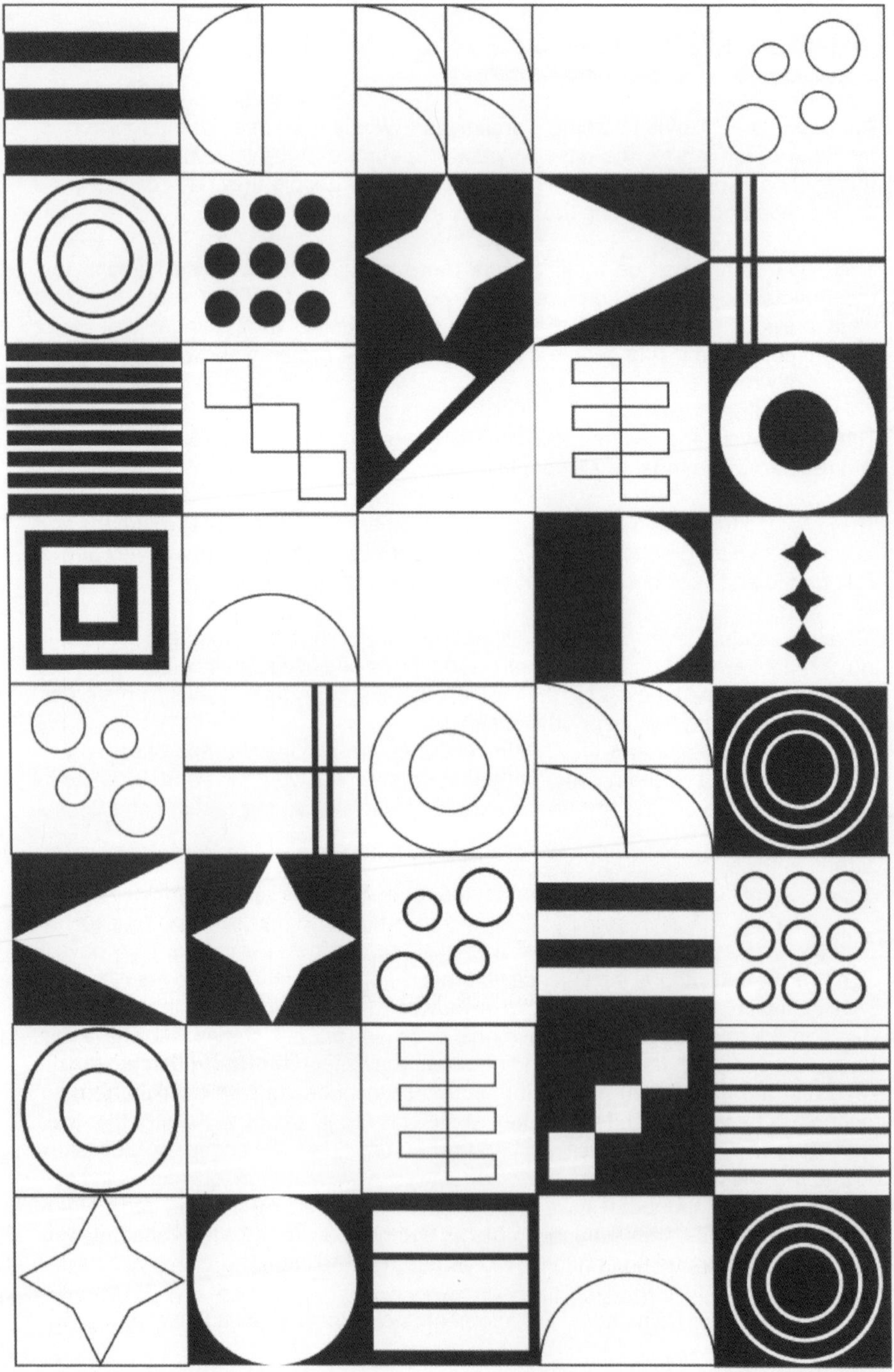

Printed in Great Britain
by Amazon